JESUS INSPIRED

Poems Photo's And Songs

Shareka Marbra

Dedication

This book is dedicated to my children. Never stop chasing your dreams. Whatever plans that God has for you pursue them with your whole heart. With God all things are possible if you believe (Matt. 19:25). Mommy loves you guys.

Acknowledgment

I would like to give all honor, glory and thanks to God, who is my life, my love, my Lord, and my Savior Jesus Christ. Without him none of my accomplishments would be possible. He has been a constant presence in my life even when I was not aware of him, and I thank him for always being with me and sustaining me throughout my life's journey. God is love, try him!

Thank you to my husband, Alvin Marbra (Pastor), my cousin LaShaunda Davis (Prophetess), and my mom Tracy Stewart, for always encouraging me to pursue all that God has for me. Dreams do come true if you humble yourself and submit to the will of God. I love you all.

Contents

POEMS

Shareka Marbra

You're Safe

There's something shinning within your core

Dying to let out a big roar

I can see all the pain that you've endured

Trust me when I say I have the cure

Your heart I will protect

Nor will I never neglect

I'll be with you always

Until the end of time

My love for you is unfailing

No need to decline

For this is only the beginning of something new

Let not your heart trouble you

For I have come to shake the ground and pave the way

When walking with me there's always a new day

His Love

The tears I shed are tears of joy

The tears I shed because there's pain no more

The tears I shed brings peace to my soul

The tears I shed make room to be whole

Every drop that falls is restored with strength

Every drop that falls causes me to repent

Every drop that falls is heard through my cry

For this very reason I will never deny

Your existence, your power, your grace, and your love

It is you my sweet Lord I adore up above

The tears that I shed, I shed them no more

You have given me strength to continue to soar

Your grace is sufficient I will abide in thee

Because you were always abiding in me

Shareka Marbra

My Everything

You gave your life for a dying world

Who never understood just what kind of pearl

You were and still are, there's none like You

Who continues to love us even though You new

Our hearts would be troubled

Our minds not at ease

One thing I know is Your love supersedes

Everything we have encountered You've endured it all

To my knees will I fall to reverence You King

My mouth will confess you are the Supreme Being

Mighty and powerful my father You are

That Glorious Shinning Morning Star

You Made It

You are now among the cloud of witnesses

where you have longed to be for some time

I can hear you now cheering us on

as you did while you were in line

waiting for that special call to hear Our Father's voice

He said you did not have to worry any longer

My child you have ran your course

The seeds you have planted will not go unnoticed

In return a harvest will be reaped

God smiles at the work you have done for Him

Just as a baby when He first leaped

Our hearts are saddened

It is true, you knew

That someday we would have to face

This journey without you here with us

But thank God you finished your race

No more pain no more suffering

You are safe in God's loving arms

At ease, your soul is resting

Where everyone hopes to be

Shareka Marbra

Keep shining your light like the Jewel you are

For all of us to see

We love you grandma

There's Hope

As hard as it may seem

That many things in between

Your life can change in an instance

From your struggles to your dreams

From balancing life, and sometimes what seems

To be a never-ending battle

Do not ever lose sight

Of the One who is always there

Holding you afloat

Because He just simply cares

About your highs and your lows

Your beauty and what beholds

The future He has planned for you If only you could see

That God took His time

When He thought of you and me

He said that you were a conqueror

That you could stand the test of time

He said that you were not fearful

Because you knew that He was on your side

He said that you were powerful

Because you accepted Him to lead

You into a place where battles are won

So, victory you received

He said that you were full of wisdom

Knowledge that came from up above

That is why you do not have to carry

Those burdens you sometimes hug

Let them go and look to the hills

Where your help truly comes from

No matter what you go through

He will always be the One

To come rescue you in a time of need

Superwoman you do not have to be

That is the reason He died for you

So that you could truly become set free

A Prepared Place

The one who seeks

Is prepared a place

The one who endures

Will finish the race

The one who is blameless

Will see the Lord

The one who lifts Him up

Will be drawn to thee

The one who surrenders

Will be in perfect peace

The one who loves

Will inherit the land

The one who's foundation

Is not built on sand

Will whether the storms

With God's mighty hand

While you are here

Make the best of your days

When Christ returns

You shall be amazed

Be fully persuaded

That the Lord is near

To receive your crown

That soon will appear

Humble yourself

Unto the hand of God

And watch how He works

To give you a fresh start

A new creation you are

For the world to see

That God did a work inside of thee

Incomplete you are

Until Christ returns

What a day that shall be

Who is brighter than the sun

My father in heaven

Whose name pulls weight

The time has come

For you to relate

So that you do not end up in

The fiery lake

Heaven is real

It is the place to be

Where we will be united

With all of thee

Shareka Marbra

Quietness

As I close my eyes to slumber

My spirit speaks as if it were thunder

I know that sound all too well

As my Father urges to get my attention

While the enemy has no way of prevention

I quietly humble myself unto his hand

All powerful and mighty is He

Hearken to His still voice

As to what His plans shall be

The outcome is already established

As He knows what is best for me

His thoughts are delightful and intriguing

Something I could have never imagined them to be

As I delight myself in His presence

Surly goodness and mercy shall follow me

I arise with a burning fire

Trickling from within

Provisions are beyond bountiful

As clear as sparkling seas

My heart is filled with joy

He supplied all my needs.

Shareka Marbra

Compass

We are all guided by the truth

that lies within thee

Darkness is his habitant

His radiance shines for all to see

While storms may try to consume us

He strengthens us for the test

When we feel that we cannot go on

He provides a place of rest

The enemy is constantly pursuing us

Intending that we should fail

But victory is always delivered

Through His supernatural mail

When we fail to follow directions

He reroutes us with His love

We will never have to question

Where our Source comes from, up above

As He take us through a journey

Undeniably secured in Him

We can be sure of our destination

Because it was always residing with Him

Shareka Marbra

Unawareness

We often brisk through life unintentionally

Forgetting the Source of Life who helps us to see

As the wind blows and the tress begin to sway

Our sense of awareness is sometimes blown away.

When the sun shines and rest upon the mountaintops

The beauty of His splendor and all its vast arrays

Are seen throughout the world as it slowly begins to decay

As the raindrops fall a forest begins to sprout

Just like life inside of us when we relinquish all our doubts

For every breath that is given it is taken without a thought

Unaware of the Life Giver whose Spirit we often blot out

It is foolish to think that we were not created beyond his means

An incomprehensible God who made all things that were unseen

As you come into the knowledge and awareness of our King

My prayer for you today is that your eyesight becomes very keen

Do You know Him

There is a man who was sent to save us

This man took upon the sins of the world

There is a man who was beating and downtrodden

Only to give up His life because of love

There is a man who never complained

When obstacles were put in his way

There is a man who knew his purpose

This man pressed His way all the way through

There is a man who knew no sin,

This man was perfect He was blameless He was true

There is a man who invites us to live with him

In paradise if we accept Him, we will be new

This man is still alive today

In spirit form I already thought you knew

When this man comes back to redeem us

What will the outcome be for you

Shareka Marbra

Do you know this man I speak of

He was here before time as we knew

This man's name is Jesus

Will you accept him so that you can make it through

DREAMS AND VISIONS IN PICTURE FORM ATTACHED WITH SCRIPTURE

Shareka Marbra

Holy Spirit

God is a Spirit: and they that worship him must worship him in spirit and in truth.

John 4:24

Fruit of the Spirit

But the fruit of the spirit is love, joy, peace, patience, kindness, goodness, faithfulness, gentleness, self-control.

Galatians 5:22-23

Shareka Marbra

Wind of God

But they that wait upon the Lord shall renew their strength; they shall mount up with wings as eagles; they shall run, and not be weary; and they shall walk, and not faint.

Isaiah 40:31

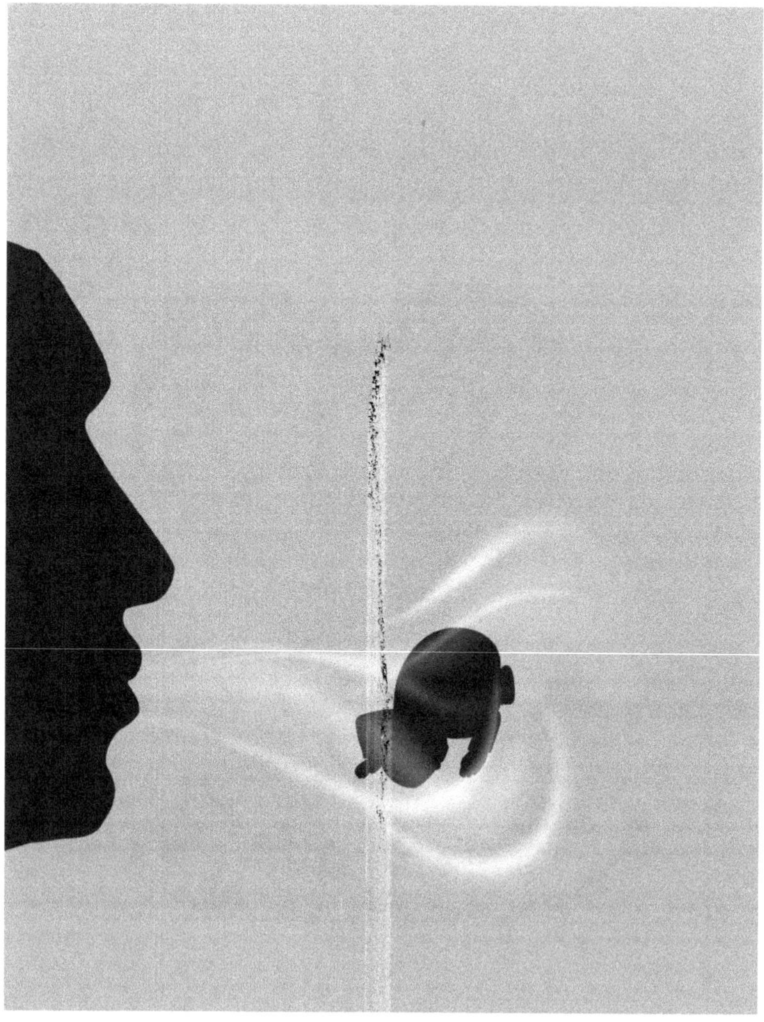

Faith Comes by Hearing

So then faith cometh by hearing, and hearing by the word of God.

Romans 10:17

Shareka Marbra

Let the Children Come

Jesus said, "Let the little children come to me, and do not hinder them, for the kingdom of heaven belongs to such as these."

Matthew 19:14

She has Strength

She is clothed with strength and dignity, and she laughs without fear of the future.

Proverbs 31:25

Angel Guards Heaven

After he drove the man out, he placed on the east side of the Garden of Eden cherubim and a flaming sword flashing back and forth to guard the way to the tree of life.

Genesis 3:24

Crown

I press towards the mark for the prize of the high calling of God in Christ Jesus.

Philippians 3:14

Shareka Marbra

The Lion of Judah

The Lion of Judah has overcome.

Revelation 5:5

Holy City

I saw the Holy City, the new Jerusalem, coming down out of heaven from God, prepared as a bride beautifully dressed for her husband.

Revelation 21:2

Shareka Marbra

SONGS

Lift Your Name High

We will lift your name up high

We will lift your name up high

You will place our feet on solid ground

We lift you high, higher

You will never leave our side

You will never leave our side

Cause your faithfulness is justified

We lift you high, higher

All my trust is put in you

You're the only one who could get me through

All these trials, my hope is in you

We lift you high, higher

But now I know, there's no one like you, Lord who makes me whole, we lift you high

And now I know, there's no one who can satisfy my soul, we lift you high

And now I know, there's a place in heaven made for me to go, we lift you high

And now I know, no devil in hell can take me back on that road, cause we lift you high, higher

We will lift your name up high

We will lift your name up high

You will place our feet on solid ground

We lift you high, higher

You will never leave our side

You will never leave our side

Cause your faithfulness is justified

We lift you high, higher

All my trust is put in you

You're the only one who could get me through

All these trials my hope is in you

We lift you high, higher

But now I know, there's no one like you Lord who makes me whole, we lift you high

And now I know, there's no one who can satisfy my soul, we lift you high

And now I know, there's a place in heaven made for me to go, we lift you high

And now I know, no devil in hell can take me back on that road, cause we lift you high, higher

We will lift your name up high

We will lift your name up high

You will place our feet on solid ground

We lift you high, higher

Bless His Name

My soul loves Jesus

My soul blesses His name

My soul loves Jesus

Bless, bless His name

He is my rock, in the weary land

He is my shield, so I can stand

He is my fortress and my portion

I'll bless, I'll bless His name

My soul loves Jesus

My soul blesses His name

My soul loves Jesus

Bless, bless His name

My salvation the gift of life

He is the Star the Morning Light

He has his hands on my soul

He is the thunder the lightning pole

He is the one who makes me whole

I'll bless, I'll bless His name

My soul loves Jesus

My soul blesses His name

My soul loves Jesus

Bless, bless His name

Jesus loves you oh Yes, He does

Jesus loves you oh Yes, He does

Jesus loves you oh Yes, He does

Bless, bless His name

Shareka Marbra

The King was Born to Live

Glory hallelujah, oh glory hallelujah

Glory hallelujah the King was born to live

He washes me from all sin

He washes me from all sin

He washes me from all sin

The King was born to love

His faithfulness no one compares to Him

His faithfulness no one compares to Him

His faithfulness no one compares to Him

The King was born to live

His patience no one so fortunate

His patience no one so fortunate

His patience no one so fortunate

The King was born to live

Hallelujah We Praise You

Hallelujah we praise you

Hallelujah we praise you

Hallelujah we praise you

Your Holy Name

Hallelujah we praise you

Hallelujah we praise you

Hallelujah we praise you

Your Holy Name

(It's not about us)

It's not about us, we praise you

It's not about us, we praise you

It's not about us, we praise you

Your Holy Name

(You get the glory)

You get the glory, we praise you

You get the glory, we praise you

You get the glory, we praise you

Your Holy Name

(Heaven on earth) (Heaven on earth) (Hellelujah)

Heaven on earth, we praise you

Heaven on earth, we praise you

Heaven on earth, we praise you

Your Holy Name

 (He's high lifted up)

He's high lifted up, we praise you

He's high lifted up, we praise you

He's high lifted up, we praise you

Your Holy Name

Oh oh oh

(Say)

Hallelujah we praise you

Hallelujah we praise you

Hallelujah we praise you

Your Holy Name

Jesus, Jesus, Jesus

You are enough, we praise you

You are enough, we praise you

You are enough, we praise you

Your Holy Name

(oh how we cherish your love)

We cherish your love, we praise you

We cherish your love, we praise you

We cherish your love, we praise you

Your Holy Name

Holy, Holy

Holy holy, you are so holy

Righteous righteous, you are so righteous

Perfect perfect, you are so perfect

Your Holy Name

(Say)

Holy holy

Holy holy, you are so holy

Righteous righteous, you are so righteous

Perfect perfect, you are so perfect

Your Holy Name

Holy holy

Holy holy, you are so holy

Righteous righteous, you are so righteous

Perfect perfect, you are so perfect

Your Holy Name

(Hallelujah)

Hallelujah we praise you

Hallelujah we praise you

Hallelujah we praise you

Your Holy Name

Shareka Marbra

Victory Belongs to You

Victory belongs to You

Victory belongs to You

Victory belongs to You

Victory belongs to You

So here I stand

Standing on Your Word

Trusting your commands, that You'll make all things work

You'll never leave my side

You'll always provide for me, for me

Victory belongs

To the ones You love

You gave a perfect son

To conquer the world

His life they did not take

It was never a mistake

Cause you knew, you knew

That victory belongs to You

Victory belongs to You

That victory belongs to You

That victory belongs to You

That victory belongs to You

That victory belongs to You

That victory belongs to You

Victory belongs

It belongs to us

A little lower than the angels

So, it's You I'll trust

You're Mighty and You're Sovereign

You'll always keep on loving on us, us

Cause victory belongs to You

Victory belongs to You

Victory belongs to You

Victory belongs to You

Victory belongs to You

Victory belongs to You

The victory belongs to You

Cause you knew, you knew

So here I stand

Standing on your Word

Trusting your commands

That you'll make all things work

You'll never leave my side

You'll always provide for me, for me

Cause victory belongs to you

Victory belongs to You

Victory belongs to You

The victory belongs to You

The victory belongs to You

The victory belongs to You

The victory belongs to You

The victory belongs to You

Holy Holy

Holy holy, the Lord God Almighty

Who was and is and is to come

Holy holy, the Lord God Almighty

Who was and is and is to come

Holy Holy the Lord God Almighty

Who was and is and is to come

Holy holy, the Lord God Almighty

Who was and is and is to come

Holy holy holy, our God reigns

Who was and is and is to come

Holy holy holy, our god reigns

Who was and is and is to come

Holy holy holy, our God reigns

Who was and is and is to come

The Alpha and the Omega

He has come to save us

And give us salvation

For our sins he died

So you will never have to try

To walk alone

Just come on home

Holy holy, the Lord God Almighty

Who was and is and is to come

Holy holy, the Lord God almighty

Who was and is and is to come

The gift of life

It's free to receive Him

Just trust Him obey and believe Him

Confess it with your mouth

Believe it in your heart

That He was raised front the dead

And you will be saved

He'll never steer you wrong

Life with Him is where you belong

Holy holy holy, our God reigns

Who was and is and is to come

Holy holy holy, our God reigns

Who was and is and is to come

Although your life

May have many struggles

Just hold on He'll never let you go

Sometimes it may seem

That the enemy is free

To do what he wants

To tear up your home

But we're singing

Holy holy, Jesus is the lamb

All powerful and mighty is His hand

Holy holy, holy Jesus is the lamb

All powerful and mighty is His hand

Holy holy, holy Jesus is the lamb

All powerful and mighty is His hand

Holy holy, holy Jesus is the lamb

All powerful and mighty is His hand

Nothing can consume you

Cause He is always with you

Take back your power and use what's within

Holy holy, the Lord God Almighty

Who was and is and is to come

Holy holy, the Lord God Almighty

Who was and is and is to come

Shareka Marbra

Holy holy holy, our God reigns

Who was and is and is to come

 Holy holy holy, our God reigns

Who was and is and is to come

Who was and is and is

Who was and is and is

Who was and is and is to come

Hallelujah I'm Free

When I think about His goodness

And what He's done for me

I say hallelujah, my soul is free

I don't have any doubt

That He'll work all things out

I say hallelujah, my soul is free

He has done great things

Great things for me

I say hallelujah, my soul is free

He has brought me out

From darkness to His light

I say hallelujah, my soul is free

He has made me ruler

Ruler over much

I say hallelujah, my soul is free

When the devil comes and tries

Tries to take my life

I say hallelujah, my soul is free

Jesus is my life

For me, he died

I say hallelujah, my soul is free

I don't have to worry

My God is worthy

Hallelujah, my soul is free

God's Got It

Don't you worry about a thing, God's got it

Don't you worry about a thing, God's got it

Don't you worry about a thing, God's got it

Don't you worry about a thing, God's got it

Time out for worrying (worrying)

Time out for stressing (stressing)

Time out for thinking you belong in this world

Time out for sleepless nights (sleepless nights)

Time out for hopeless flights (hopeless flights)

Hard times they come to see if you believe in what He says

We are all just passing by (passing by)

We were made to worship Christ (worship Christ)

What's meant for evil He'll make it right

If you abide in His Word

Author and finisher of our lives (my life)

Obedience better than sacrifice (that's right)

With Him, everything will be all right (all right)

Don't you worry about a thing, God's got it

Don't you worry about a thing, God's got it

Don't you worry about a thing, God's got it

Don't you worry about a thing, God's got it

Don't you worry about a thing, God's got it

My Hero

(Nothing brings me greater joy than to be able to sing this song to
my Lord and Savior Jesus Christ, Hallelujah)

You're my hero

Just as far as I can see it

Cause when I'm going through these cycles

You came and gave me help

And nothing can compare to

All the love and grace you share

That's why I have no problem saying

You're the air within my breath

Jesus, you're my hero

You're my hero

Jesus, you're my hero

You're the air within my breath

There's no time to waste

He'll set you free

Just get on your knees

Once you believe

He'll make you new

Once he gets through with you

Jesus, you're my hero

You're my hero

Jesus, you're my hero

You're the air within my breath

Jesus, you're my hero

You're my hero

Jesus, you're my hero

You're the air within my breath

No time to waste (No time)

He'll set you free (I'm free)

Just get on your knees (Cause 1 believe)

Once you believe

(I'm new) He'll make you new

Once he gets through with you

Jesus, you're my hero

You're my hero

Jesus, you're my hero

You're the air within my breath

You're the air within my breath

You're the air within my breath

(Then the Lord God formed man out of the dust of the ground and breathe into his nostrils the breath of life and man became a living soul)

You're the air within my breath

You're the air within my breath

You're the air within my breath

You're the air within my breath

You're the air within my breath

You're the air within my breath

You're the air within my breath

I Just Want to See You

How amazing is it that God sent His only Son into the world not to condemn us but to save us.

Sent from heaven

There up above

I just want to see you

I just want to see you

Like no other

There up above

I just want to see you

I just want to see you

You're rocking and you're rolling

Convicting and patrolling

I just want to see you

I just want to see you

Not one of us is worthy

But you came and called us worthy

I just want to see you

I just want to see you

Sent from heaven

There up above

I just want to see you

I just want to see you

Like no other

There up above

I just want to see you

I just want to see you

No matter what the world says

Jesus, you're the one who's perfect

I just want to see you

I just want to see you

And when that day finally comes

United with the true Son

I just want to see you

I just want to see you

You were sent from heaven

There up above

I just want to see you

I just want to see you

Like no other

There up above

I just want to see you

I just want to see you

You're rocking and you're rolling

Convicting and patrolling

I just want to see you

I just want to see you

Not one of us is worthy

But you came and called us worthy

I just want to see you

I just want to see you

Sent from heaven

There up above

I just want to see you

I just want to see you

Like no other

There up above

I just want to see you

I just want to see you

You're rocking and you're rolling

Convicting and patrolling

I just want to see you

I just want to see you

Not one of us is worthy

But you came and called us worthy

I just want to see you

I just want to see you

I just want to see you

I just want to see you

I just want to see you

I just want to see you

This book was inspired by God and breathed by the Holy Spirit. This book was created to remind people that God has not stopped speaking. He speaks in many ways. This book is filled with poems, dreams, and visions in the form of pictures and copyrighted unreleased songs that were given to me by God. He is the same God, and he never changes. I pray that this book inspires, encourages, and pushes someone into their full potential and purpose in God. If you have lost hope in your dreams and desires know that your God-given gifts and talents are to be used for His Kingdom. Someone in the world needs their fire within stirred back up for God. Release what God has put inside of you so that it brings Him glory. Pursuit for God is everything. By the grace of God watch your fruit grow into fruition because of your obedience. God Bless.

Shareka Marbra

About The Author

Shareka Marbra is a wife, mother, minister, worship leader and a devoted servant of God. She has always had a kind heart, gentle spirit, care, and concern for people. When she received salvation in 2018 her passionate heart and love for our Lord and Savior Jesus Christ began to pour out of her even the more. Her passion and love for God's people is inspiring and empowering. She has always made it her duty to encourage people and bring joy and peace into the lives of those she touches. She is a lover of God's word end enjoys spending time with family, singing, writing gospel music and uplifting poems that point people to Christ. She is a respected leader in the church she attends and loves serving those in her community. The life that she lives is a testament to God's glory and she gives all praises to him alone.